Something & Nothing

Also by David Lindley

POETRY
Poems
The Night Outside
Five, Seven, Five

PROSE
Ideas of Order
The Freedom to Be Tragic

Something & Nothing
Selected poems

David Lindley

Verborum Editions

© David Lindley 2013

First published 2013 by Verborum Editions

Verborum Editions
5 Lauds Road
Crick
Northamptonshire
England
NN6 7TJ

www.verborumeditions.com

Set in Janson

Book designed by Sarah Rock

Cover photos:
Front cover: David Lindley   *Back cover:* Claire Louise

978-1-907100-01-7

Contents

Something & Nothing
7

From a Year
95

Repeating Myself
157

...

Editorial Note
188

...the human genome project has shown that worms and people are sufficiently similar at a genetic level for meaningful inferences to be drawn...
The Economist 26.05.2001

I

Something & Nothing

GHOSTS

I keep in touch with one or two
old ghosts. In winter, when my feet are cold,
I think of peasants stuffing straw in their boots,
hoary frost on dead chrysanthemums,
water frozen in the rain butt
and poets cut off by snow-covered lanes.

Unthinkable, the drifts of books piled up,
so many lives tumbled together,
so many springs and summers
and a thousand winters iced up in there,
waiting for the thaw.

AFTER THE WAR

Coming home after
the war he asked a stranger
to point out his house.

Spring, and everywhere sparrows
are nesting under the eaves.

WORDS FOR EMPTINESS

All that can't be said
may not be said
in words that mark
this page with furrows
but must be said in spaces
in between these
blackened lines
that make
emptiness apparent.

SOMETHING AND NOTHING

There's been a disturbance
outside, some shouting,
fighting, voices raised.
It's over now,
the silence of the long dark
night prevails. It was,
she always used to say,
something and nothing.

JUST THE SAME

Realising how things are
though not so numerous
just the same
we're just the same
like flies
alighting somewhere
looking for something
how shall we find time
between us
to whisper such longings
that between us
will suspend the afternoon
for one another
and the hum of evening
dying down?

THE APPLE TREE

The apple tree
planted by the long since dead
torments me in the wind
in croaking syllables
with memories of severed limbs
and hacked off branches, complaining
of its impotence now that its meagre
sprigs of leaves bear nothing
much, much occupied with pity
and the inescapability of guilt
passed on from one to
one another fruitlessly.

SONG THRUSH

Were you finally to loosen
all the bonds of flesh and knowledge
(you think the birds do now,
arced across the sky)
and free yourself to be as they are,
were you to leave it all
to sing full-throated on the apple bough
and then without a thought
wheel upward, homeward
through the scented air,
how little you would know
of air and freedom, knowing only this.
Listen. Repeated blows of snail shells
hammered on the stone, the flung
shell and ripe flesh, flurry of wings
and then the sudden stillness of the night
are raptures of the real
from which there is no flight.

WINTER BALACLAVAS

Click, clock,
the long
grey needles
tucked into
her arms like
extra limbs,
her fingers
moving at a rate
of – knots…

Click, clock,
she knits the ribs
of winter balaclavas,
ravelling and unravelling
all that is to be
and all that's
endlessly unfinished.

Her eyes measure me,
her fingers knit and knot
and click and clock
all that will become of me.

NOT TO END

Poems and prayers
are both
for the same
end
to keep the same
the same
and not to
end.

PRESENTIMENT

Walking up the Euston Road –
pains in my chest –
a pigeon flew into my face
batting my eyelids closed with its wing.

Nothing in my book of omens
tells me what this thing
might presage
but I doubt it's a sign of grace.

SYMPHONY

When you came
to write your
ninth
did you think
perhaps

yes

that it would be

yes

your last

yes
I hoped so

but you

yes
I went on living.

THE LONG HAUL

Apes evolved
to stand upright
in line
at airport check-ins,

learned, in fact,
to fly

like Ariel

to Carib isles
once westwardly imagined
by an earlier chimp

who picked
preserving words out

one by one
with sharpened goose-quills,

the way
we used to do
with straws
poked into termite hills.

THE NAME SHE SAID

The present – all we have –
uncertain as a rickety stair
dimly lighted, and we
who bear the names
she named herself with love
she greets as semblances
of others long since dead.

She talks of lamp-lit
streets and walks
defiantly to meet him
past the hour when she's
expected home in bed
a presence here among
her ghosts – the name she said.

CLEMATIS

Clematis blows
unhinged in the wind
recklessly acrobatic.

Once the air is still
the tendrils waver
and edge into chance
encounters with the sun.

The eye too catches
at something tangential,
a leaf, a cloud, a blackbird, crow
like the hand finds a finger
commanding beginnings.

What else can I cling to
what can I know
but love and the day
and such things they proffer
blindly, tenderly seized on?

LAST THINGS

I thought again of days
too perfectly bucolic,
that pastoral effusion
that hangs like mist
above the ribbed remains
of open fields
where sheep graze.

I watch the crows
unearthing worms,
those celebrants
of absences.

What is experience?
What do I know?

Nothing of nothing,
only something,
the one last thing
the last man knows.

THE MIND IN WINTER

My mind still lingers
over leaves to clear
and frost to come

while everything
else moves on
in one direction

hyacinths in a bowl

birds I saw puffed up
against the cold
now sleek and busy
with beginnings

but I'm intent
on what I've left behind
ignoring signs

not ready yet
for hope
and indecision

winter at least
has a kind of clarity
and cold precision.

SECOND BIRTH

Birth is a prelude
waiting for the day
like mayflies hatching
in the month of May
for the sudden sweet
rush into being
when seeing is
too much to say.

WHAT HAPPENS

Yesterday
I saw that
blossom lay
like snow
along the apple
bough and

now today
I see that
snow lies
on the bough
like apple blossom.

Is what happens
in the world just this
interplay of words?

FLAPPING

Washing flapping on the line,
shadows flapping on the grass.

The blackbird flaps its wings
to fly

forever pegged
to earth and sky.

A BOY IN CHURCH

The best parts were
the stained glass sunbeam motes
and the dying organ notes
which meant you could get out
of there
and back into the sun
where the sacrifice we'd heard about
had only just begun.

NOTHING DOING

So isn't this
the virtue of it all
to have done nothing

since silence
was the one thing
we agreed upon

right at the beginning
whenever we spoke
of where it would all end?

NOTHING AND SOMETHING

I looked through every crack
to see where nothing hid

but something stared me back
just as it always did.

IN THE DARK

After millions of years in the dark
life decided living was the only way
to appreciate the novelty
of always being dead.

THE HOUR

If all the dead
could live another
hour it would of course
be this one. That's
quite a responsibility
for the living.

METAPHOR

I love trees
as analogies,

but birds
can't find words

for what a tree is for
without a metaphor.

STICKS

I saw him
floating sticks
under a bridge
hanging on to the railings
among the traffic
on that small island
where only immortals live.

CLOWN

At nine he ran away
to be a clown.

In dreams he floats
above the town

in buttons red and blue,
a hero and an angel

hereabouts who left
the right way for the true.

THE WORLD'S INDEFINITENESS

I never learned the names
for plants and animals, reassured
by my vagueness of the world's
indefiniteness.

From memory
I pick up words and try
them out – clematis,
camellia – which is which? –

hydrangea and geranium, one
pink-eyed reliant on the soil's
acidity to stop it turning blue
as one despondent

gardening column
correspondent learned,
like shellfish
keep flamingos from becoming
Spanish dancers.

Words are only good for conversation
and never touch the world itself
where every blade of grass
possesses its own silence.

So what am I talking about?
Nothing really.

NAMELESS

Unless you call me
by my name

I'll wander down this
street for ever

rustling the leaves and
ruffling your hair

until you stop
and turn and stare

wondering who it is
who isn't there.

THE MERMAID

She too
wants to know,

her legs fused together,
a mermaid,

what it's like
to walk out

into the miracle
of day and why

we are allowed.

HER POEMS

She set them up as little temples
we might worship at with words instead
of stones like truth and spirit.

Oh, no, they haven't tumbled down,
she made them well in spite of time.
You'll find them if you look for them

in drawers with birds' eggs, shells
and necklace beads,
needless basement things.

THE AFTERLIFE

After
the rain
the sun
       you see
we are already
living
in the afterlife.

HUNTERS AND GATHERERS

He was a hunter
of triangles
and came home
empty handed
most days
I gather.

ROMAN RUINS

The ruins are deserted.
What did you expect,
to see with the eyes of centurions?

You're not their memorial
any more than you had
a place in their imagination.

Take it from me
we have only each other's
absence in common.

NEIGHBOURS

A lawn is supposed
to be level, not undulating –
supposed, since an ideal
lawn is already presupposed.

Neighbours tell me
there's too much moss
and the thistles, though neatly
cut, are deep rooted,
and a roller would help
flatten things out.

But I won't do it,
because this is a lawn
of a different order and
hasn't the first idea of
what a lawn should be.

It was in some place like this
I discovered the spring's first
crocus, got shot several times
in a friendly way and recovered,
sat in quiet contemplation
on a mound, once
wrote a poem, squandered
my soldiers among the uncut
blades of grass,
and may for all you know
yet march
my discontented army out
across a heavenly uneven field
all unsuspected.

PARROTS

> *See, he answers*
> *nicely when he's spoken to.*
> Elizabeth Bishop

She was driving
through Rio
with the back full
of parrots
shipping out the worst
of them no one
cared where
when the Jeep stalled
and a policeman
sweating
yelled at her
to get this heap
of shit off the road
shoved his arm
through the open window
fumbled at her breast
and started the ignition.

Thank you officer!
Fuck you!
Asshole!
Turd!

FUGUE

Fugue the Sorbonne.
Fugue the Café Cluny.
Fugue the bad cheese sandwich.
Fugue the grey Parisian drizzle.
Fugue Sviatoslav Richter.
Fugue Bach.

HEAVEN AND HELL

Nowhere is it written
and since the pains we will suffer
are uncertain and the place unknown
we need not imagine it
or believe it.
The choice is simple.
Wait.

STUDY

The ape muses
in bronze
thinking how far
he has to go
to get here.

TREE

The sapling staked

tree that was
tree that will be

battling together
the winter wind.

THE SOUL MAKES HEADLINES

'Apes
too
have souls,'
says
primate.

TRUCK

Not one of those old
poets would believe
the way we live
driving at eighty
miles an hour.
But they'd recognise
the flat-bed truck
of hay and straw.

WHEN SHE DIDN'T TURN UP

When she didn't turn up
I caught the last bus
to Hatfield's for a drink.

Give up women, he said,
poetry is more certain,
bashing out a single line

on his old typewriter
as though by beginning
we could write a different ending.

THE ASSASSIN

We wake
and the cold light
stabs us in the heart.

We are afraid to go out.
The trees are shattered
in the wind
and morning runs through the street
like an assassin.

ADVICE

Don't choose a wife
in the dry season,
look for a woman
with a fat behind
in the fat season.

Build your house
with the right wood
in the wet season.

Dream of caterpillars
for a good caterpillar season
and don't change your shape
without a good reason.

APPLES

Raking rotten apples
among apple leaves
got me thinking

what the essence
of an apple is
what point of ripeness

marks the apogee
of an apple
the distance travelled

out of nothingness
to be the thing
I call an apple

that now shrinks
back from being
into abstract

retracts from appleness
to other
to something

that the wasp
appreciates
the blackbird finalises

nothing more
than a man
thinks of.

FEVER

I smell gunsmoke
in the air
and know
thunder
is coming.

At last the fever
breaks.

Light headed,
I am somewhere
on a mountain
under pines,
gathering berries
in the rain.

They are still
shooting people.

THE SURVIVOR

She said
it was always peaceful
like this
the forest blue green
behind us
everyone quietly
going about
their business
piling up bodies
burning them.

THE EXECUTION OF AN UNKNOWN WOMAN

If there are reasons
the true colours of them
are hidden in the wood
now the snow has fallen.

Millions of creatures in the forest are never seen.
They live out their lives in the night.
The bird of paradise flaunts itself before dawn
and flies off in morning's half-light.

Beauty is unreasonable,
squandering flowers at midnight,
unnumbering stars on the other side
of the wood, out of sight.

LOST

At dusk
the starlings
drop to roost together

as souls
like leaves
anonymously gather

and at some signal
from the night
are glossed

with starling wings
whirled up in winds
and lost.

ANGLE

The angle of the leaning
fence among spring flowers
underneath a tree
is just the way
the things that are
should be.

EVENING PRAYER

A dull man
when the day ends
should pray to live
and make amends.

HIEROGLYPHS

Snow falls
through the night.
Dreams come.
Awake
I think in my own way.

The wren
who lives in silence
behind the tangled vines
has written in the snow
the hieroglyph for absence.

My thoughts fall
through the world
until I vanish
and the wren
becomes a leaf.

RADIO SILENCE

Confusion of signals
not loud but insistent chatter
like an alarm of birds
product of an inner torment
hard to place.
Stomach acid perhaps.

Doesn't seem to interfere
with the usual predictable
patterns of behaviour
mating, birth, mutual
hostility and death.

It's pitched high
to the point you'd call it abstract
continuous as cicadas at evening.

Some things come through.
Love and do you
death and must you
frantic between them
in the constant anxious hum.

Eventually they destroy themselves.
I've seen them crushed beneath stone
their essence washed away
in the changing seasons.

From here I still can't tell
if it's blood
or formic acid.

But the radio is turned off.

AT THE ROADSIDE

Dead flowers
and forgotten notes
of their avowals.

What can you expect
from a language afraid
of its vowels
and
the elemental
but
the sentimental?

NIGHT

For you
in her bed
the night
is too short
for me
alone
unending.

EVENSONG

I'm travelling at speed
along the road
inside a steel capsule
but radio waves catch me up
in time for Evensong.

God of my fathers, God
of the mountains and the plains,
do You ever get used to
this sort of thing, God
of stillness and silence?

HELLO AND GOODBYE

Sap bursts
into leaves
as blithe in
tremulous green
arriving
as they are in leaving
waving red
and brown handkerchiefs.

CHAOS

Ripped clouds
lose their defining
edge to the grey
sky that has no
beginning or end
and like the incessant
rain must stand collectively
for something else
undemarcated.

How can I say
that one thing is
and not another?

The worm edges into
the blackbird's nature
and the bird takes
sudden flight
protesting its name.

ALL SAID AND DONE

The berries are bright
on the holly
in the sun.
The birds alight
on the holly
to eat the red berries.
There,
it's all said and done.

BORN 1945

I

Recompensed with innocence,
ha, ha. As if they
didn't know from Adam
being born is an act of guilt.

They did it furtively
anyway, the green light
filtering into that bedroom
through leafy damask curtains
an arbour for no good.

We're up to the hilt
in it, life, and life's the thing.
The dead lie doubled up as
yellowing sheets of underlay
carpeting an imagined wood
where children play
and birds are too afraid to sing.

II

To believe her
nights were spent
stumbling about in the dark
saying excuse me,
the days waiting to see,
awaiting the relief of absence
and what was to be made of it,
falling into darkness finally
at three a.m.,
that hour of excuses
for crying out loud.

THE TWO MARYS

As thought there were some perfumed balm for this,
she thinking, how am I supposed to feel?
Yet how easily the two of them have settled in the house
together, so now you can't tell them apart.

The days have lengthened but there's no more light.
The table where they'd eaten last is covered
with a new cloth and rugs on the floor hide
the marks of his feet across the carpet.

Dressed and composed in the brown colours
of earth and sacrifice she waits for the opening
of hyacinths on their spinal columns and the news
that none of this is true, waits for reports of him
seen wounded and ashamed walking towards her.

LADYBIRD

Do not accompany me
I don't want to wear
your heart on my sleeve.

Colourful and dotty as you are
my madness is my own device
though the white page
attracts us both.

Leave
and let me write
ladybird.

I DIGRESS

I digress
of course
off course
it's those
lanes waymarked
scenic
routes that
reassure me
there are
other minds
up to no good
taking the long
way through
the wood.

THE IMPOSSIBLE

> *Outside, the same dark snowflake*
> *seemed to be falling over and over again.*
> Charles Simic

Every snowflake is
supposed to be different
though each one looks
like the same one falling.
You'd have to run
and pick them up one by one
and see for that to be
more than mathematically probable.
Closing my eyes and holding
out an open hand I don't know
what they are
tricks of the light
touching me in the dark
becoming impossible.

NOT YET

One bare thought
stopped me dead.
Yes, that was it,
like a cold draught
under the door
while I was busy making
a skeletal construction
of bright steel arms
with wheels and pulleys
of perpetual motion.
It was the first
appearance of that notion
as hollow and empty
as the wind
that swept under the door.
My mother must have heard
it too for she looked at me
and said, Not yet,
my love, not yet.

CASSANDRA

Those were the days
when gods moved
not in mysterious ways
but as you and I do
a comical set who
fooled around since the gods
have no fate
but plenty of history
of course which is why
you don't run into them
often though once
I caught a glimpse
of a grey-eyed goddess
on a bus and there was
that wild-haired woman
who called to me as
I was getting into a taxi
as if to warn me
from one who understood
civilisation and the capacity
for abstract thought
would bring me no good.

ATTENTION TO LESSONS

There was always a forbidden
area, the window itself
for example, as if nothing
could be learned
by looking out when
so much yet remained
to be remembered,
out where the field ended
and the hill began, up to
the crazy line of posts
that marked the quarry
boundary. And not to go
near the edge where the ground
gave way to heady space
and not to scratch at the grain
that runs through wood
a wavering line to London,
Paris, south to Marseilles
and a boat perhaps to
India, depending how far
you could get on
disobedience and inattention.

DELI

I kept going to the deli
just to look at
the girl who worked there
and the way she gathered
her hair at the nape
of her neck and hesitated
wrapping a loaf of bread.

On the way back
I met friends
who said I don't really
need anything but
I'm on the way to the deli
I may just pick up
a loaf of bread.

ROADS

Ah, the roads
I've travelled
night after night
overlaid on one another
all heading for home
like worn out tyre treads
trampled underfoot
in the snow
no telling any more
which way to go
or if anywhere they lead to
would be any place I know.

I'm no more certain
what the signs say
awake than dreaming
always lost and always
looking for somewhere familiar
I've never been before
and someone waiting
and someone opening the door.

CRIME AND PUNISHMENT

In the water-closet of eternity
pages of the News of the World
hang on a nail, all they are fit for
my father said, though he read
every one of them looking for the truth
and not believing a word of it.

The wind howls through the cracks
in the door and under my arse
so I know there is something else
out there, but for the present
I've only a random assortment of words
waiting to be washed out to sea
and the spider in the corner
hanging by a thread.
O, spider, intercede for me.

HYPHEN

A thrips
singularly singular
has found itself
in the bathroom,
a tiny black speck
in an expanse
of white porcelain.

Outside
the hot August sun
has bleached the sky
white as a basin.

A hyphen
high as a kite
connects to
the infinite.

THEIR EVENING AWAY FROM HOME

So the conversation went
the fire smoked in the grate
meanwhile back at the old homestead
the video recorder quietly whirred.

RIDDLE

What knows
and knows nothing,
is innocent
and guilty,
never speaks
but is always eloquent,
signifies meaning
and its absence,
ends as it begins,
is all that I was
and all I must be?
Silence.

THE BRIDGE

Mid-twentieth century
and men are delivering
coal on their backs
and rain is falling.
All day I have wandered
in the municipal library
where Greek islands
of translucent air
await a ship out of the blue.
Outside under the rickety
railway bridge bleak engines
black with smoke
push resolutely onward,
the bridge crossed homeward
clouds with steam
and for a moment
everything rises.

LEAVING

Not one
but many
not numberless
but one
slipping from something
into nothing
as easily as falling leaves
we are as numerous
but not to be grieved
for being many
but only
for being one.

BEACH HOUSE

...an unfamiliar time of year.
The Guardian, 17 November 2012

November is an unfamiliar month
a dubstep and grime
swindle for the 808
trigger fingers of trap
that fills your head
with hazy memories
of the summer fling
you didn't have,
the samey fallback position
of Balkan-esque melancholia
like a seminal digital mystic
sipping a mojita
on a concrete walkway.
There's still room in the beach house.

CHAIRS

> *The chairs were bored…*
> Marc Chagall

The chairs were bored,
but look how they arrange themselves
expectantly around the lecture hall
rising to the occasion,
waiting as empty spaces
always do for something,
a gift, a straw hat,
an encouraging word from you.

PIGMENT OF THE IMAGINATION

You say no one could
have imagined this
layer upon layer of dust
creating the illusion
of a peacock's eye
that colour should be
in the world
you imagine
like the unknowable blue
pigment of the sky.

PIE IN THE SKY

The apple lies
at the foot of the tree
its eye pecked out.
Too many blackbirds
to take it for a pie.

NIGHT LIGHT

At the end of the street
past the streetlight
life's in full swing
but I'm looking in
through the window
from the night
that is quiet and still
and I can't
no I can't
I can't come in.

ANGELS AND MESSENGERS

The mind in the form
Josef Herman

Something winged
before it was a bird
the wind against
my face
in the night
the mystery of the air
moving unbidden
the unseen
among things seen
when I close my eyes
did I invent all these
the abstract bird
sweep of shingle
angels and messengers
crying to be let in?

A NOTE FROM CEZANNE

Madame
I'll never embarrass you
by pointing out
to anyone
the apples
that still shine
where you rubbed them
on your petticoat.

HISTORY

And so I go on
year after year
century after century
my memory failing.

MORNING

> *In the morning it was morning*
> Charles Bukowski

What happened
to the dream of me
after the night's
long struggle,
what am I doing here
when I left yesterday?
It's infuriating
having to start over
again putting all
that stuff in order.
Let's see who I am
tomorrow.

II

From a Year

Winter.
Nothing much
to distinguish it by
not even
sea from sky.

New year.
If you should think of it
just now something
will surely begin.

Lament
for the world's
lost equilibrium:

I am
therefore
nothing
no longer
is.

The present
is mostly
absence.

Last flower,
late bee.

Where now?

What is there
before or after
experience?

Everything waits in the dark
for you to say

Come in.

This is
the natural history
of the mind.

I open my eyes
and the birds are there

their wings pinned
to the blue arc
of the sky.

In the field of rape
yellow butterflies
are invisible.
Me?
I'm just passing by.

Enough
that the cold is ending
that something is stirring
underground.

At the side of the road
molehills
their northern slopes
covered with snow.

Under the ice
the fish are hidden
even from themselves.

Birds flee the snow,
black arrows,
craw, craw.
Hens hide from it,
red feathers,
squawk, squawk.

One moment
something
vanished

the next moment
something.

No words
for the surprise

of birds' feet printed
in the snow.

They're written
for me.

Bees
buggering about all day
among the promiscuous orchids.

I never said I loved you.

What do I know?
Who asks?

A is for Absence
B is for Being
C

Bats skimming
flies at dusk

with nothing
to go on

but echoes
of the real.

Morning.

I am always pleased
to find myself here

and know that the time
when I am not

has nothing to do with it.

Now we've moved
to a house
with windows in
the sloping roof
when I pee I watch
the crows fly by.

The silence
hums
buzzes
chatters
ill at ease with itself.

O
this perpetual
is

The day departs
of course
without me.

Whatever it was
I was thinking of
vanished.
Full moon,
flight of swans.

Under snow
the fields
are a white canvas
the trees
painted here
and there.

The cow that grazes
grazes.
The man who sweeps leaves
is out sweeping leaves.

Eternity is
a single room,
a bare light bulb.

Everything in the end
decides in favour of spring,
puts out new shoots,
opens its eyes,
croaks, chirps
yes.

Rain at the window,
first light of morning.
How long, how long?

Clouds drift in the water.
Suddenly a fish jumps
out of a blue sky.

The sun shines,
the wind is chill,
clouds hurry by.
We hear nothing
but lies.

This is my fate
to wake each morning
and never to know
not waking.

It is spring only
because something unceasing
calls me by its name.

This is the book
I was reading
that day
they came to arrest me.

Pigeons in the square
as usual.

How could one bear
to live for ever?

It's unfinished but
take the painting anyway.

What does finished mean?

In the undergrowth
the corpse of a headless toad.

Ah, now it is known!

The priestly smell
of candles extinguished

like something accomplished.

I regret
coming this far.

The endless streets
vanish in the rain.

In a corner of the shed
rows of chrysalides

waiting to become
something else.

In the garden
she labours
in striped pants

free for a while
among leaves.

I meditate on
the ultimate truth of things.

Sparrows peck at seeds.

Night never begins.

Moon outside my window,
lamplight in the courtyard.

The year ends,
another begins.

Still it is not finished.

Every time it snows
I am back again under
her window
waiting.

Ice and snow
slow down
impetuous thoughts.
One
has to think
one
step at a time.

You
departed
weep
(you can't)
for all the things
you can't
weep for
I can.

My hand trailing
in the water.

The frog and I
surprise each other.

Footsteps in snow,
words on white paper.

Something made,
something spoiled.

In the room they stand
talking to each other

waiting for me to go.

Sitting in a dry lav,
emptiness of fields.

O, the perilous voyage
of my bare flesh
through cold winds.

Boats made from walnut
halves with paper sails.

All still endlessly voyaging.

I lived among books.

Sometimes I thought of the sea
and a ship's siren.

She lives her life but

I know the taste of her lips
better than she does.

Fallen chestnuts
fail the promise
of beginnings.

Weeds grow high
in the hedgerows.

Those who love life
believe only in beginnings.

Waking to snow.
The lightness of the moment
has drifted into years.

FROM A YEAR

Winter

After a night of storms
unbroken by the wind
snowdrops.

Spring

The earth bears
everything
even your sadness.

Summer

When the page was blank
no one thought suddenly
a flower will appear.

Autumn

You hurry home
to match the landscape
to your box of colours.

THE LIFE OF STONES

I am
as they are.

Let them
speak.

III

Repeating Myself

ONE NOTE
> *From* Lucretius, *De rerum natura*

I haven't much to say.

Better after all
to look up suddenly
at the sound of swans
calling overhead
and watch their disappearing flight

than have to listen
all day long
to the clangour of cranes
heading north
contentious among clouds.

SEVEN POEMS ON THEMES BY ŌKUBO SHIBUTSU

To give up medicine for poetry,
to doctor these poor patient
words into imperfect verse
has been my malady,
lingering here at the mountain's side
with my patent cure for melancholy.

I can't afford to buy a place with a view.
I've one room shuttered with a blind
that keeps out the street noise
but lets in the moon.
My books are piled on the floor.
Lying here in the moonlight
I can see all their titles at once.
I'd like a Chinese ink-brush painting
to hang on the wall where distant
mountains and lakes will appear
from just a few brush-strokes.

Through the heat of the summer
I didn't think of a single poem,
as though someone had broken into
my restless sleep and run off
with my dreams.
One day I woke up suddenly
in the cool air with an idea
in my head
only to find the birds
had got there before me.

On a boat
listening to summer insects
each with its own voice
joyful or grieving
their sounds
drive out my thoughts.
Farther from the shore
they become
one distant song
of farewell.

Rain and wind
in sudden squalls,
the road a river,
bamboo scattered
on the grass
like torn feathers,
butterflies contending
hopelessly, more off their course
than usual, a trellis
of red blossom
taken all at once.
Undeterred, the birds
swoop down to pick
up mud and broken twigs
to build their nests.

Cicadas in the trees at sunset.
Suddenly, wind and lightning.
Clouds hide the mountain,
the rain is already crossing the river,
the swallows not yet home and
my books about to get wet.
Yet all evening
I've been sitting in the cool air
unable to write a single line.

FINDING RHYMES FOR FISH

From what's left in the autumn
garden plot a few dwarfish
potatoes and a purple
aubergine sliced will make
a tasty salt and olive oil dish
with a glass of wine – say
around seven-ish.

IN IMITATION OF A POEM BY ISHIKAWA JOZAN

Cherry blossom scattered
on the lawn at evening.

The spring and I
both feel old.

I can't say
you betrayed me.

When the blossom
was on the tree

I was the one who
forgot to look.

BASHŌ TRAVELLING

Nine days to Ichiburi
up and down
with sweat and dysentery.

Awake all night with the bugs
biting and the horse
pissing in my ear.

No sleep again
trying not to hear the whores
whispering through the wall.

Arriving home
one's own gate is like something
remembered from a dream.

FROM THE CHINESE OF WEN TING-YÜN

A cock crows.
Straw
outside the inn
the moon
on the wooden bridge
footprints
in the frost.

COLD MOUNTAIN: 17 POEMS OF HAN SHAN

She's a real beauty they say
hidden from view behind a curtain.
You'd compare her skin to peaches or pears.
In the east the spring mist rises,
in the west the autumn winds.
Thirty times over and there's just the pith
with the sweetness squeezed out.

A bird has settled
in the mulberry tree.
Moving, it has a grace of its own,
singing, it sounds just right.
Is all this for me? Who else
is here to delight in the day
but the singer and the one
who dances?

Lost, the way to go.
Long, getting there.
Chirp, the birds.
Still, no one here.
Sharp, the wind.
Drifts, the snow.
Day, like night.
Years, without spring.

The days go by
as though they were drunk
and had stumbled past.
Pushing up daisies
you won't see the sun.
Once your bones have dried out
even your ghost
will get tired of waiting.
Born again as a horse
you'd be champing at the bit
for a book to read.

Life and death
are like
water and ice
first one thing
then another
and nothing
to choose
between them.

Here mountains and streams
follow upon each other
and the clouds stay close to the hills.
In the morning mist
my hat and coat get wet.
I'm wearing my old walking shoes
and carrying a stick.
The world seems like a dream,
forgotten already.

Yesterday – walking along the path
among peaches and plums.
In a garden a girl
in her summer dress,
so beautiful I wanted to call out
but couldn't speak.

People today are pasty-faced
and vacant but say
they don't have a care in the world.
Ask them what they care for
and they can't reply.
I thought I understood emptiness,
but…

Sitting alone, too bad,
my thoughts – too sad.
Mist on the mountains just lies,
wind in the valley just sighs.
Monkeys in the trees, jabber jabber,
birds in the woods, chatter chatter.
Another year, hair grey and straggled,
older, sorrowful, more bedraggled.

Cold Mountain always
surprises the traveller.
The moon shines on the water,
the wind sighs in the grass,
bare trees have snow for blossom
and clouds make do as leaves.
After the rain it's so fresh and clear,
just right for climbing higher.

Once I was poor, now
things have gone from bad to worse.
Nothing worked out
and I went downhill.
I walk about in the mud
on old bent legs
or sit holding my stomach.
Since I lost the grey cat
the rat comes looking for leftovers.

Living on Cold Mountain
for all I know thousands of years
have gone by.

I left the world
for woods and streams
and sit here
with a clear mind
to which nothing clings.

Cold Mountain, where no one comes –
white clouds, that never leave,
grass for a bed,
sky for a cover,

happy to live
pillowed on earth
watching things change.

On Cold Mountain
everything else ceases.
I wander along
without thinking
writing a few lines
here and there
living the floating life.

Words for food don't appease hunger,
words for clothes won't keep you warm.
If you want to eat – eat,
if you're cold – get dressed.
If you don't understand,
thinking things through
just makes it harder.

No use looking for it –
turn around and it's there!

I don't need to own this mountain ridge
to belong here among the white clouds.
To get through the passes you need a strong stick,
to climb up higher you hold on to vines.
In the valley the pines are always green
and streams cascade brightly over stones.
No one comes by to say hello,
only the birds in spring. Tweet, tweet.

Free among mountains,
nothing to detain me,
nothing I need do but live
and think as I like.
Now and then I take a book
up to my rock-strewn palace.
Below, the abyss, above, the clouds.
The moon is cold, the wind sighs,
and I'm here like a lone crane, flying.

I keep repeating myself
like a crazy old man.
Do I offend you always
telling things as they are?

Crossing over to death
you'll wonder what all
these words were for

and what kept you.

EDITORIAL NOTE

The poems in this collection are not arranged chronologically, but arbitrarily, like their origins. Some have appeared, sometimes in slightly different forms, in other places: *The Times Literary Supplement*, London; *Poetry Durham*, Durham University; *The Magazine*, Warwick University; *People to People*, West Midlands Arts; *Raw Edge*, Birmingham; *The Haiku Quarterly; Red Lights*, New York; *Lilliput Review*, Pittsburgh, PA; and in earlier collections now out of print – *Poems; The Night Outside; Five, Seven, Five*, all published by Salvo.

www.ingramcontent.com/pod-product-compliance
Lightning Source LLC
Chambersburg PA
CBHW020802160426
43192CB00006B/402